FRIENDS
OF ACPL

READING POWER

Oscar de la Hoya
Gold-Medal Boxer

Rob Kirkpatrick

The Rosen Publishing Group's
PowerKids Press ™
New York

1

To you, the reader.

Published in 2000 by The Rosen Publishing Group, Inc.
29 East 21st Street, New York, NY 10010

First Edition

Book design: Maria Melendez

Photo Credits: pp. 5, 11 © Simon Bruty/Allsport; p. 7 © Ken Levine/Allsport; p. 9 © Holly Stein/Allsport; pp. 13, 15 © Al Bello/Allsport; pp. 17, 22 © Stephen Dunn/Allsport; p. 19 © David Cannon/Allsport; p.21 © Mike Powell/Allsport.

Text Consultant: Linda J. Kirkpatrick, Reading Specialist/Reading Recovery Teacher

Kirkpatrick, Rob.
   Oscar de la Hoya : gold-medal boxer / by Rob Kirkpatrick.
   p. cm. — (Reading Power)
Includes index.
SUMMARY: Introduces the Mexican American boxer whose skills won him a gold medal in the Olympics.
   ISBN 0-8239-5543-5
   1. De la Hoya, Oscar, 1973– Juvenile literature. 2. Boxers (Sports)—United States Biography Juvenile literature. [1. De la Hoya, Oscar, 1973– 2. Boxers (Sports) 3. Mexican Americans Biography.] I. Title. II. Series.
   GV1132.D37 K57 1999
   796.83'092—dc21
   [B]

99-16068
CIP

Manufactured in the United States of America

Contents

Oscar de la Hoya is a boxer.

Oscar grew up in Mexico. He lives in the United States now. Oscar likes Mexico and the United States.

Boxers throw punches. Oscar can punch with his left hand, and he can punch with his right hand.

Boxers wear robes when
they go in the ring. They
wear gloves when
they box.

Oscar likes to go to the gym.

13

Sometimes boxers sit down to rest. They sit down in the corner of the ring.

Boxers get belts for big
wins. Oscar loves to win
belts.

PALA

17

Oscar boxed for the United States in the Olympics. He won a lot of fights.

Oscar won a gold medal in the Olympics.

Oscar just loves to box.
He is a good boxer.

Here is a good book to read about Oscar de la Hoya:

Oscar de la Hoya: A Real-Life Reader Biography
by Valerie Menard & Valene Menard
Mitchell Lane Publishers (1998)

To learn more about boxing, check out these Web sites:

http://www.boxingonline.com
http://www.delahoyafanclub.com

Glossary

belts (BELTS) What boxers get when they win fights.

corner (KOR-ner) The place in the ring where boxers go to rest after each round.

fights (FYTS) What boxers do in the ring.

gloves (GLUVZ) What boxers wear on their hands.

gold medal (GOLD MEH-dul) What you win when you are the best at a sport in the Olympics.

Index

Word Count: 125

Note to Librarians, Teachers, and Parents

If reading is a challenge, Reading Power is a solution! Reading Power is perfect for readers who want high-interest subject matter at an accessible reading level. These fact-filled, photo-illustrated books are designed for readers who want straightforward vocabulary, engaging topics, and a manageable reading experience. With clear picture/text correspondence, leveled Reading Power books put the reader in charge. Now readers have the power to get the information they want and the skills they need in a user-friendly format.